Honest James

Christian Schlegel

The Song Cave

Published by The Song Cave
www.the-song-cave.com

Cover: detail of *The Beekeepers and the Birdnester*, by Pieter Bruegel the Elder, 1568
Author photo by Sara Deniz Akant
Design and layout by Mary Austin Speaker

ISBN: 978-0-9884643-8-4
Library of Congress Control Number: 2015931471

FIRST EDITION

for my family

Table of Contents

I

I

Play, Muse, upon my pain, so that your playing
nobly causes in my breast to swell another strain
more adequate to this, my task of marking time.

GOETHE

Little Ballad

Come gather round me, goodmen ten,
as dims the pale I've ambled through.
I store mine eyes in a baking tin
and shelve it skew.

A wreath is a lay is a chanterelle
beside a gutted bream and bread;
come gather round and bid me tell
that I am dead.

Three coreops from arbor drear
will suit my grave as soon it's dug.
Wet them with tears and carry your cares
in a calfskin rug.

In mine are packed a hundred sighs
to blow me fast to the house below
(O children of Reading, would I were wise)
and down I go.

Der Zauberberg

One friend asked, haltingly, if my confinement could be halved
before a taller friend, a banker bred on Schiller, laughed
and praised the villa's "mineralic views."
They each agreed to sit beside me through the ice of summer
and the warm December.
It was not news
when uncle fell again.
My cousin came with papers
for an August or an April train
to see the man in Bonn.
Only the moon appeared to set. I lay and did not choose.

Fable

A melancholic pastor, paraphrasing
a psalm of David's, cribs from a pantoum he knows:
"the lining of the cape he shows
to those assembled dazzles—mendicants . . . an earl . . . a vole,
and they are changed." The pastor's boy is lazing,
composing on a lyre:
"The rain lifts. Shining fire
will baffle men disposed to retroversion of the soul."

The linen of the cape he shows is dyed
in pink and sepia, and there are scenes of boys
asleep, hugging their lyres. This noise
inside the organ-pipes before they're tuned determines how
the pipes will sound beneath the note that's tried,
and strained. The sadness lifts.
And girls remain in shifts
who want to change. A hog is eating slop beside a sow.

That is the note. The burgermeister writes
a line of casuistic doggerel in chalk,
intended for his wife. They balk
at making love. An envoy calls and stays past coffee-hour,
reciting children's verse: long-bearded wights
dozing among the dead
and kindred sprites. The red
imposter has a little book, he says, and reads it in his tower.

For Ben

1.

What you have risked, I too,
but haply I, unhaply you.

2.

The magister in Mandalay—short, souverain and saintly—
will offer each the martinets a Martinican floret, and bouquets of lime.

They are drying and drying faintly, the bouquets of mint and lime.

3.

Vary does the dolor but the laughter pricks forever after,
loquor, ego loquor, meo voce atque spiritu.

Safe is the malingerer, and dafter. An ailing man is safer.
Loquor, ego loquor, meo voce atque spiritu.

4.

Do you love me, brother,
love under the pitch and pother
the draff of me? Or

are you loving-dust and I a bother,
a blatherer: knowing you worry there, and begging you hither?

5.

Wroth the rose the light's forsaken,
light and lighter dart the hares,
I am by the post you placed, with counting-books about me
    and a jug of beer.

Harried are the drakes, their sleekness
rare though I expect their sleekness,

near the Dorset briar with my counting-books and beer.

A Thought of Saint Paul's

I shall bring along sin, saying, "It is my sin,
of a body and soul, and a part its own."
I shall pray on this brown
hill as dawn wings in.

Diptych

1.

I put on my coat with its Labrador collar, straight and stiff.

Words will approach actual things, drift this way, anagram,
parataxis, aphorism, syrinx, color, this way.

Implication and figuration, our primary constraints,
play no part in it.

On March 5th I catch a dark maid roaming a fusty, half-dismal
bog. "I must stay in my locus purus," Samantha gasps, climbing
a birch, gray frock dangling.

Day and night pass. A month will pass. An owl lands on a low wall.

Indigo is diving toward dusk.

That dark maid is lost to you—for you, a spirit, insist on loss.
Having only your habits for succor.

2.

A bonanza of fruits and rolls, rum and brandy, gorgonzola, slick
fish from Monday's haul . . . scallops, broccoli, gold onions
in a bowl brought from Spain . . . .

This imaginary painting transforms into a spatial list, a grammar
for moving through.

I was born so, arguing about a quality of hail, not hail as such,
das Ding an sich. I am not afraid of doing anything.

That lithograph of a narwhal, its tusk bursting from turbid foam,
drags us away. But a cornucopia is constant, containing nothing
but its possibility.

I will hold your black pumps, soft with rain, as you pad around
in stockings. I will kiss your brow. I will do this knowing
I cannot again.

Now I am thinking of my family . . . now a Sardinian man tilts
a milk-pail. Milk is trickling down a cant in his floor.

Rhubarb and garlic, bananas, Cornish roast. Almonds,
Brazil nuts, raisins, filling an iron bowl.

Klaxons spill into this fabulous night.

A Quality of Portugal

Is . . . is . . . .
The 21st, late in the year, we are all sitting and you
have abandoned Tom Caruthers
(uh-huh, we know about it, and for Samuel
    with the droop-shoulders)—
you are in that era of high silliness,
Trotsky-on-toast!—we can't stand the thought
of one another. Even the televisual support system
of the laser light-show purchased by the Donovans
(they are always . . .)
overwrought, all of it. Tiddling about the new Anchises-
and Hector-themed plate sets they had installed
in the second kitchen. Night-birds
diverting in their little divorced warble to the stars,
even the stars are amused, everything is droll,
there shines a liquid beneath us smooth,
but it isn't polite to point that out. Oh monstrous me
we are in the pool again, oughtn't we be scandalized.

Inside the flambeaux-pink dining console
Morton has decided, bosh, it's going nowhere,
my children are mush-handlers and toadies.
This isn't Cleveland. There were rules
in the previous way of things. Uncle Cimilon, the hostess waves, won't
you pass through the foyer and grab us another

tray of something? Turns. I've been wanting to talk to myself
in *your* presence
in this ashen robe for some time.

Tough everything. I have an announcement, Bob stammers
(no one can bear his fascicles of glee),
I have cornered the raccoon near the side portico,
won't the guests please lend their attentions . . . .
Oh how touching, Tippie-darling . . . .
Really! It's something else when he
massages you, I could swear he was whispering
in my ear the whole hour,
I spend long weekends imagining,
I kept asking—
do they speak Spanish there, where you're from
are there beaches
and like an old friend
he didn't nod, didn't disagree.
He just held me.

Pictures of C. S.

I was not hale as a younger man,
but now I'm stout and the labor's fine
I suffer anew, for the light of six, the active light,
is a pox to me.

I came one eve to a drawing boy
of a foreign mien in the market-fair
and he drew by the silver-light of nine
the black of my hair.

So I took to myself and I kept thee away—
we had not time nor common aim—
and the midnight-glow of the clouds and snow
was never the same.

How I Wrote Certain of My Books

A Bunch of Flowers for Girls

Moth's-root for Mathilde, afflatus-leaf for Rosa . . . .
Oh, and something of Cynthia's choosing, a broach
joining these fallen wastes
to aeries smelling of lavender.

Bathers in Arcady

A rill runs in certitude from the hilltop.
A gloaming gives way.
A smooth, impassive wanness announces its plainness.

Locus Solus

"I think my improved mood is attributable to three factors.
First, I am eating better, though not so much as is recommended.
Second, there is a new steadiness of concentration . . . ."
The notebook ends here.

A collage of Dalmatian elms. The turnip-farmers blench
at a stand of lightning.

"The Chair-Sized Man"

Some time it is, now, to be a man born of men
and not of green, and quiet.

Bathers in Arcady (II)

In me there is not flare nor flower nor form of flower.

The girls in bunches are fresh and unextinguished,
doubled in clear view, "their bodies like guitars."

Impressions of Africa

The hunter too young in his khakis.
The parlor is stuffy, and dragonflies wind through the atrium.

The Blackbird

Climbing up to the carillon we sang like rogues,
and danced and tumbled along the wall,
and the boys below pressed cider.

Later we parted. When my father died
I took up his several rooms on Libauer Strasse
and painted after supper.

The Lady from Portugal, Grigia, Perfection of a Love

"Thank you for joining me on short notice."
The doctor spoke through a mustache
into the Austrian noon.
Towering trees.
Little quiches, table-wine for a picnic.
Ascomycotina, *Senecio alpinus.*

How I Wrote Certain of My Books

Many have asked, what is the good in making the new lake
(though not so many as I'd have hoped).

The new lake, of course, is deeper and farther from town,
and girt by a broad path.

A Golden Age Passes to a Silver Age

A house turns to a cave but in daytime. There is pollen in the air.

The drapes are pulled back.
The queen is inside where you left her.

Dostoevsky

"Then suddenly the scene changes and some sort of 'Festival of Life' begins, in which even insects sing, a turtle appears with some sort of sacramental Latin words, and, if I remember, a mineral—that is, an altogether inanimate object—also gets to sing about something. Generally, everyone sings incessantly, and if they speak, they squabble somehow indefinitely, but again with a tinge of higher meaning."
—*from* Demons

In the earlier version of the vision one swings over that serpentine
regress of thinkers bent at their sky-paintings, sea-paintings,
beach-paintings, hazel and ermine, caramel and coruscated:

men who miss home and the care of their wives and mothers;
men who are nearly boys but who shave and wear trousers.

And in the snowy arts encampment maybe one in twenty
stands up to the scrutiny of the elder, a Cossack in his forties
with the memory of a beard.

The writer for whom the vision is present remembers the elder
and his fan, but the earlier version has him reclining, *being* fanned.
And nothing alters in the long haul,

a messenger comes anyway, hesitates for a minute,
trips over his wings.

Design describes.

The shape and thickness of the waves, the cock of your head,
the slope of your impossible frame at the breadbasket, where you
make something quick to take with you for the journey ahead—
the dog already on the corner laughing with her tongue out,
sweating into the air—

the air describes.

We could say we were besotted, unable to complete what we had
started or had meant to have started. I could argue it was
a blast of powerlessness, and I laid my head in a woman's lap
and slept the course of ten dreams.

But this is the later version, when the encampment returns
to the water, and the Cossack is a panhandle farm-boy doodling
rockets on the back of a psychology exam, and we are in a lecture
theater misrepresented as the scene of the transmission
of a knowledge from times before this and onward.

Better not to argue, better not to disturb
the painters of nervous temperament, though they are men in a dream
and look right through us.

A breeze was manufactured in the Antilles and stumbled to this
shore, to this room, still smelling bright and white and fine.

And the sumptuous detail was a story on a beach hidden
from the breeze, a rock ledge with a view onto couples below,
stumbling to a shore alongside driftwood from another painting

manufactured in the Antilles, hidden from the breeze, hidden
from the couples in this room

as without detail—bathed in cool air, but an absent messenger,
and a ghost of a wing, and a sliver of night.

Are we not proud to think we have seen everything
before our eyes, the plane against which a palm tree glows
—once we were in Russia, and now we are in Florida—

and the later version is this letter, and you have read it
and will have wanted to reply, but there is an ocean here,
and no possibility of crossing it?
The night air is yours to rent but not to buy . . .

the laughter I had detected, and compared to which we were
inadequate, that was more for me than for you, for you,
was more for me than for you . . .

and was an awful feeling to sit with, but you sat with it

Epigraphs

1.

My mother shrived an oil-rig,
my father loved a squirrel,
my sister Ed was timely wed to Jane, the rakish burl.

2.

"I have not long to lie with you"—he was a red-cheeked bard—
"for I must drive to St. Paul's Inch where camp
  the Seventh Guard."
"It's nothing harsh to wait, to wait," replied Susanna Flynn,
"I'll square the grounds
and ply the hounds
then pray away the sin and shroud,
then pray away the sin."

So drove the bard by Quony Lake (the linseed flats appear),
and watered at the dented ploughs. "I know but what I hear.
I hear." He tapped his heel. "The sun is white," he hoped to say.
"An age ago
in Holstebro
I reckoned this my day to die,
I reckoned this the day."

3.

A goblin must needs eat, but never drinks.
A djinn shows teeth of nail, of nail, a tongue of peat.
The pard has louvered fins and feet with thumbs.
A rukh is wise.
And thus we are disguised.

4.

Fain would the aphorist marry Xanthippe,
and sire a dozen brooders ere his brains putresce,
his will expire.

I would a sire be
and not the lord, a husband to a holiness
but never one adored.

5.

The ensign looped a bowline with an arm around the boom,
two half-hitches cinched his britches
in the taxis of Vendome.

An aquifer will guide us to the tomb.
They bow before their niches
with their toes toward home.

6.

The bondsman's manumission brings on dire dissipation.
The freedman has no need for superstition—
  he wants for regulation
gauzed with catholic erudition.

A hawker's occupation seems a casual sedition,
netting mostly gain and good. May the gain produce elation
  and an inkling of freedom,
like the freedom in perdition from all human obligation.

Aeschylus

Peripeties obscure the prophecies
            begot of heresies in young societies,
and as societies protect the laity
            with legal probity and reciprocity
perhaps commodities and their integrity
            and the haecceity of their solidity
become the founding pieties of clerisy
            and the anxieties of later deities.

Peter

Thou readiest thyself in grace more grace to see,
may he be praised, and holy love betimes
will shew the fear thou cached. Thou grip'st that key

without a faith in doubt and with a rime
of dirt beneath thy thumbnail, red and beige, the right.
Some signs give way to signs unmarked nearer the light.

The Three Men in the One Garden

Perfect tree, perfect idiomatic tree-signifier, "this here poplar,"
for example—alongside the unproblematic sideplane of bramble
bushes, the prating dumph-flower with its photoreceptacles.
Most plants in the public garden whisper one way, then one way
again, then laugh forever and in unison. We can turn through
the terminal fructifying regions if we are agreed this is standard
protocol and content tonight in our sleep.

Is this a rutabaga I have uncovered in the sterile earth? It reflects
like a rutabaga ought. It is, however, a parsnip. Everyone was
pulling for the rutabaga, and a magical if temporary region
brimming with rutabagas, so that each could be cultivated
and before that each marveled at, and when the finished products
are numbered, dispatched we will drive to Delaware
and patronize the right establishments and parsnips do not
inspire me along these lines.

Dear lord, what we are expected to give of ourselves,
and to whom. Like the molder-heap of yams, those, by the door—
like the yam skin you have incorporated into your
complicating gestures and visions. It's only a yam's skin.

The day passes through.

Don't you wonder how many people have considered
exactly the thing you're attempting? And when you're attempting it
do you imagine yourselves all in strange communion,
and does this instance of imagination frighten you,
or does it cause you to redouble your efforts and try again,
as though you might capture that safe feeling a second time?

Eugénie Grandet

The plough today, as yesterday, turned up a golden louis in the soil.
The strength is in the creaking of the stair
        and not despite.
Outside, my father's jack (I fear the hired men) is bending to his toil.
O may our work our souls requite
        if not repair.

Jude the Obscure

"Come play with me and be my love"
I copied on the nunnery's kitchen wall
when she was out (where had she gone?), and that gray Mother
checked below the cots for bodice-rippers.

I will leave my pick and workman's glove
and bed for the spring in an ass's stall.
Grace of mine, that you return—that you return at all—
shall make my life and your devotion prove.

Pennsylvania

I spoke too much and left, and have returned
in my forgetting to this square of green,
dotted with elms, and always the elms were farmed.
I sense that I might be what I have been
and will, effortless green, blue in the night,
twinge in my arch and arm and round my wrist.
It is for being and for being missed,
and like that glory lacking it is great.
I loved it so. But I forsake it now,
not for an urgency some other place
but that the trembling (here itself) might show,
rightly to tremble as the dying trees:
    because they are still trees, they are ash-white,
    morose in happy luck, rejoicing at their fate.

Wall Park

Das Allerlei erleidete, die Blauhortensie, Esche schwarz:
I was a boy and lonely am, and give my heart.

Endlich sprang des Hauptmanns Tochter
   aus dem Kinderlied heraus.
Tousle my hair. Kiss my cheek.
Voices meek and stark disturb my father's house.

On Finishing *The Narrative of Arthur Gordon Pym*

Someone was here, an acquaintance of mine:
Paul S., with whom I'd studied as a boy
in Pennsylvania (and not long a time;
the intervening years could not destroy
completely what I now call childish joy)—
Paul S., passing through, alone, on business.
We talked in my apartment, mostly books.
"Have you read—," he stopped, testing a crepitus
in the floorboards, looking at me as looks
an engineer, though he was not,—"this thing of Poe's?"
"I have," I said, and it was true. "I don't suppose
you've read it also?" "Yes," he answered, woefully,
"I say, that book had quite an ill effect on me."
On my south wall I have an imitation of a tapestry.

"And so it had an ill effect on you . . . "
At first I only parroted his thought,
but I recalled the book's expansive blue
and, ending as it did, in white, that dot
among the snow, that whiter shade, the knot
the boy had drawn to represent the caves,
his friend whose arm rots off, whom they won't eat,
and black-toothed men with thigh-bones for their staves . . . .
"I find the novel rather over-neat,
the way one's death is neat," I said to Paul,
now looking at the empty northern wall
on which I hope to put a sketch from Cuvier.
Whatever Paul would like to say, he thinks he'll say.
The islands off Antarctica are humid, and they smell of shea.

St. Peter's Hymn

My God! my living God—I am ill-shod
for want of sense and means, though callous-footed I, for you,
will beat dead-low ten acres' land with but a switch and rood,
and ay, this too:
I'll scrip your lessons plain upon the dew.

My brother! brother shy—I'll curse the fiend
hard by in hideous mirth (O carefree sin) awaiting you.
Your word persevers, boldened by its mystery, and he is spleen
though seeming true.
And hurls he all to darkness save the simple few.

My lord! my lord at last—the chime will call
me to my knees, my grave, to paradisiac light, and you—.
My days are toys and trifles—I have fallen—I will fall
as triflers do.
King, if my inmost heart be mine, will you that heart perfect in you
 and me with love surpassing me imbue?

At the Mitre Tavern

1.

He has returned from war. Cabbage continues in the garden,
among the fist-sized radicchio.

In Italy he met a Calabrian woman and learned to read
the language.

"Dark inlets off Sardegna," he remembers hearing. "The men
wearing blue in Ostia . . . ."

2.

A professor is up much of the night, loosening a boyish translation
of a Greek poet into "boulevard speech."

"You, you, you / and in you is something fine / undaunted
by the sun / that reddens me."

3.

"Bad luck is catching," the editor tells his employees. "Be mindful
of the ocean." The four sneak schnapps onto the airport shuttle.
Sun-hats and dancing.

It is, in all, an uneventful vacation—though Sasha and Lukas quit each other soon after, and he flies back to Prague.

With sconces dimmed, Llewellyn salves his bee-stings.

4.

The student leaves his books and floats outside, to a friend.

"I spent most of the summer fixing fence. On the last day
of work, actually on the last post, I took my eye off the jamming
machine" (makes a motion like this) "and dropped it on my skull.
Ranch-hands drove me to the hospital . . . a hundred stitches . . .
my mother came out from Houston."

The student goes in and organizes his van Eyck folios,
for Monday.

5.

Dredging requires three contractors in four years.
The way the silt's moved, some of the finger-docks sit on the muck.

6.

"Our Regional Assembly is composed of two primary parties,
but the fringes hold increasing sway—demanding this and that,
pledging and withdrawing support in the newspapers."

7.

The Italian philosopher writes in his diary, "I wake early
and teach, and play bridge. I buy vegetables
near the picture-pond when it cools."

The Serbian painter waves at children from a terrace.

8.

After a decade of privation, a composer emerges from his
basement studio with a three-part score.

9.

There is some confusion as to the landau: the madam
has called for it but plans a reconciliation.

The master cannot ignore the man, once he arrives, and must
at least guide him to town, over the new high road
and skirting the fen.

But the children's trunks have been packed with care—dainties
and toys close to the top, food laid in for foul weather.

The maids turn one bed in the sun-room, throw open
the library, leave off replacing the wicks and tallow,
ask after the groundskeeper . . . .

10.

The old man daubs at grease on his cheek, while regulars stomp
their heels.

"My boy," he says, "we have a sterling future in you."

The young man slips to the lounge, and wets his hair,
and combs it through.

Fugue Composed near Boyertown

I was a hart,
a philomel, third cushion on the ducal chair, a grub,
death's practicant, right sentry by the lodge of Beelzebub,
confusion in a bowing head
that will not start
to save itself . . . the gear-lock's lip, the titan's growl . . .
    the whip instead.

I was a rook,
a Paracelsan acolyte of winsome cheer, a doll,
a fluxion . . . gases . . . porphyry, the freedom of a squall,
exasperation manifest,
the guilty cook,
ambassadors' recalcitrance, Geronimo, a tie . . . a test.

I made a strand
to live along to fill the bays I cross. I made surprise.
I made the prolongation of surprise—ennui—and eyes
to goad my thoughts into the world.
I made my hand.
A famous notion twirled and froze. I made it mine.
    Again it twirled.

I was a cod,
sweet Belgian wine, a toothpick, somnolence, an autumn weir,
the ear and tail of lynx . . . the call to raise when lynx are near,
a caterpillar wriggling in
his sopping sod,
the white between the clear, the red in gray, a squeal, a hex . . .
    a paladin . . . .

Grongar Hill

The more I dwell on it, the more trouble I have separating
activities I must complete, as an ethical imperative, from those
being merely laudable. You might object if I shirked them,
but what presuppositions are you bringing to bear, and (assuming
a baseline for required conduct) do I trust your life's worth
of tortured half-analyses in the lead-up to my decision?

It's too high a bar to clear in one leap.

If I'm lucky my wants arrive fully formed, but usually I'm in
an elegiac position (the gazebo), looking through
the wooden slats, acknowledging they are particolored, and simpler
than the earth in which they take root.

From the top the propositions I had learned dovetailed,
and had a melodic quality—
it was twilight but only just.

And my friends belonged to a countervailing
quilt of energy, rapidity,

the general description of physical features, a hamlet emitting
its digits, indicators of smoke and also of consequence, industry,
obligation, marriage. Because what was cemented between
two persons had a tiny, ineradicable impact.

Exhaust fumes leached from an animated factory.

Painters gathered to put down in impasto a landscape
before it was frittered away.
It could have remained—but it frayed.

Your mysteries of life, the hill said as it turned to my side,
are not of my making,
though really they could be . . . .

But I don't put stock in the pronunciations of the hills.
Like anyone else, they have their interests to protect.
It's not as though I fault them for it. I just don't want to be around
when someone bitterer than me, with a less developed sense
of live-and-let-live, rolls up his sleeves and gets to work.

I'm considering leaving the country.
The less room I have the more I find myself needing it.

In another country they might recognize this problem
and make it disappear.

Blackmur Pens His Coda

". . . to hasten the peas
on my desk, to find
but shape, sheer
and swooning, thought
from the seed. And so forth."
Ahem.
"Worrisome frame,
weary the brake pads. Breakwater.
Wary now in the noonday
fog becomes, fog becomes
and the hard shell within.
It is the softness without
I tarry by, tears. Tears
and the bud, the barn has
gone up, aloft in threnody
of park. Of glade."
And a quick slug. And a quick bite.
And the plum orchard,
"And, yes, and the plum orchard.
Beyond the garden is dale,
and beyond it fruit,
and beyond that the promise of fruit.
Not for now is wren
aloft. But for now is wren.
And now is air."

The New Tendency

winter had been, summer was, a train fit with people receding
throughout the meadow scattered like a card game
the data-points of people receding, forming a light stellate dust
through which the flash traveled

the house by which
the train sat heavy, fire wept in and out the windows

inside the train was the man writing
inside the forest was one thing, a yellow barn

the land darkled, grew vivid, land darkled
two cousins cobbled
insects answered low and to the wind

whatever emerged from the dark meadow found a path like music
and back to the dark meadow, and back to the old considerations,
somewhat changed

inside the train was the man writing
from Rome to Ravenna, and in this period two ideas were grown
green and velvet from the loam surrounding

a flare coughed, begetting one absent wind and two
(formerly sullen) patches of raw heat
nervous in their transmutation

oft and a rare sheen, a wilderness
between the flash and the cone deliquescing from bright lines
before them

I can say this only one way

or perhaps two ways if the first seems implausible, filled
with a solution I do not understand
but am needfully borne by, a new tendency

that is all I'm asking now, in the small span of time before (before)

otherwise I can pretend that the purple weight of this
(much of it at once) is sufficient for me
multiplying in evening and the tall grass

but soon enough we feel this isn't so

Her Poems

1.

Mill-shacks amid lingonberry scrubs.

She revises Part Four, "Catachreses of a Jotun," until 6 o'clock . . .
inserting a talking badger and ruddy provincial audience.
Vintners and chemists cycle by. Clerks have auburn-haired spouses.

The speaker unspools three Vedantic parables.

A brash youth refuses a secret . . . grows mute, makes camp
far from the mere.

He is the father of the hero in the second, an adolescent possessed
of immaterial sight and pocked complexion,
mystic given to adumbrations.

There are attempts at plainsong . . . all sepulchral wheezings
becoming dissonance.

The third relates the lives of an ancient. She calls him "halting
occiput of the warrior class." He sits cross-legged before the fire,
picks out leaves.

His yarn, of animals discussing battle in alterable-stress meter, abets uprising . . . . She ignores its parabolic structure and anachronisms (impossible vegetables, for a while; knowledge of the future).

As with others: a preponderance of windows, candles, rotted eaves, doors, chapped hands, the ocean.

The poem immediately precedent, "A Giant's Discriminations," she allows into and out of terza rima. It petrifacts into a short monologue delivered at the nexus of two rivers. Says the giant,

> Though I proceed from, unify vale and atmosphere
> the perturbations about my cuffs you call atmosphere.
> My face distends at the withering farce
> of my rhyming here . . . . The force
>
> of my footfall interrupts your performance.
> Painted bawds quake in the distance,
> plangent, aware of my standing here. This power
> is your only power.

To which she replies, "It is not unlike another. It is well-wrought. I remember an earlier sequence, someone scooting over piled barrels . . . it is left out."

2.

The new poems include correspondence.

Bits of vers libre. She interpolates the journals of Humboldt,
institutional analyses into a history of Peru, "wood-wheels
working a trail."

An abecedarian closes the first section.

Material accrues, the peaks, tunnels.

Her heroine becomes Elena, will not practice viola or borrow,
scattering chicken-feed in Lima. She kens the region's patois.

"Elena wears knickers like a stevedore, clips back her bangs."
This is the beginning. A fat hound parades and is footnoted,
signaling cathexis.

Elena was reared without sisters high on the craggy reef,
where came her lover silent as death, bearded,
his back to the harbor.

But father disapproved. Sea bludgeoned that fragile plaster.
She was sent to the interior to study;
he hiked to Parana, so humid is Parana.

And the haibun goes

for even if   was he   However   stray the sun . . .
and passion   was he.

46th Street and West Avenue

So Thomas, also styled Didymus,
dreamt from Sidon nigh unto West Capernaum
addenda to Leviticus
regarding special cleanliness.
"The unclean must not rot nor else be known,"
  he spaketh to his friend,
"non sic harmonium
sit omnium
in caelo. Tu es omnis. Tu
es sacrus. And the tidings of our prophets may
  some suffering forfend
but never judgment—that is sure.
One weeps but shall not rue
and rarely sleeps, but works, loving the work,
  and loves the sinner more."

When Goethe saw the lord he held him fast,
through fits of holy ardor. Yea, his God was man
without man's pique. Said he, "Du hast,
nichts habe ich, du machst 'ne Faust,
you go where list you go and I shall walk behind, touch thy blue hem
as touch I can.
A vain Corinthian
abides in me; I am his host.
But God is goodly jealous and his wrath will life secure.
    Woe unto them
that seek. I will not seek. Amen."
Evening. Soft as a ghost
the lord declared, "Verily I will comfort thee
    till all is dark, and even then."

Honest James

Oh well, I am my master now . . . The step,
the tamped-earth track are mine . . . and I cannot be lost.
If dreams I had in boyhood they were dreams
of this, walking alone. Crabbed, pink-veined and swelled,
aged forty-four, I keep the light in me.

That is the hill where he is gone to disappear, my little lord.
I do rehearse at night, at home with Sam, the early shame,
my failures as a man she held not to account
and such a man I do not mark today.
My father read the sermon when we married were and mother laughed.

You, William, take the bond of me I offer you,
I give it fast and mostly free . . . ah, yes, brown wool,
I thought this was your scarf—it has a hole—you could
not run away. Leave off beside that spike
of fence and I will soon to warm your hand, to lead you back.

You will have cried believing you were dead
(I dreamt once that my teeth and neck were teal.)
Curse neither luck nor beast that brought you here,
boy that I've raised and found, boy that I would were James.
Look to—pick up the reins, press with your spurs.

I give you peace—lean close, lean to the horse's mane. Have peace.

II

Goethe: Variations

Spot of Time

Ach, Eros, there you are! Or I see your hands
          at least, uncommon fine, and by them both an hourglass.
Capricious god, more imp than prince! Let pass
          the hours. Quicken life, or what I hope is life,
               —and still the sands.

The Four Seasons

TULIP: I am the connoisseuress of myself.

I: 'Tis fair, I said (ignoring her mistake)
—and more sense lies in a tulip-bulb
than in the leaves of the books I've bought
that crowd the shelf.
And yet I cannot give my books away,
and you grow sentimental.

TULIP: Aye, for I must grieve myself
before I die,
for I am grown to grieve.

I: Am not I too?

TULIP: You are the connoisseur of much that is yellow
and some that is true.

Cannot differentiate between the cloves before me:
some I love and some abhor.
Am all for cloves (adored, unloved),
carnations, blue nasturtiums, weeds that overcome the garden-floor
but do not overwhelm, as they have choked the cloves before.

Admixing my hunger, my desire for color,
with the image of the beet at my elbow,
I set off to plant the beet of my eye in the earth
and exchange with the wind its symbol for my sound.

Here, a desk of manuscripts, but am no scholar.
Impart my will upon the men before me
    but can have no power.

You began,
"I wanted to have everything, and with you everything to share
    (*but that was there*);
I wanted to bake bread for you and eat sardines, fourscore and ten
    (*but that was then*);
I clomb the sea and swam the cliffs of marble shear
    (*not far from here*);
tarry with me, tarry with me
    (*and tell me, will it fully and forever be*)."

Does dawn, embarrassed at the scent of flowers
it has stirred to living in the day to come,
lie closer to the night—it does—or day—
to what extent—and so the likeness fades . . .
does dawn, the sky's first, inner dome, lie closer to itself—
it can—and who will intercede on dawn's behalf—
the light—the aster-plant—the Persian vines,
and of this intercession is the dawn ashamed—

A memory:
Mephisto turned to greet the moon,
and both saw twinges of red thread, matte,
  coursing through his beard,
and Gretchen swooned.

And you replied:
I have two friends,
the first a Helion, the light personified,
the second Phoebus Apollo,
and at his command the sun is said to rise.

The Monday I turned seventeen I met my boyhood friend
and ran with him beneath a highway,
Lancaster, Monocacy, where else we ran
(I'm tempted now to say "straight through the cemetery,"
but we went at evening-pace along its side),
Kutztown, the local airport, Tulpehocken,
Cumru Township, Blue Marsh Lake.

These the intermittences I found in the Pacific Sea:
my anger and impassiveness,
the desultory nature of my reading and my passion for it,
jealousy and superficial ease
as demonstrated for the sake of friends
(I felt I must perform myself to save my friends).
The west was thus. The east engendered nothing,
in the eastern sea I'd merely bathe.

Quiet avenues, winter potatoes, spring spargel, summer potatoes,
the Oberbaum Bridge. From our roof we watch a fantastic yellow
hulking contrivance ten blocks toward the river, and say
to each other: a contrivance pummels the earth, my dear,
and the earth is the sorrow it feels. And the bat beds down
on the back of the sow, and the brook falls asleep on its heels.
Occasionally a friend arrives to add a stanza.

The whistle of blue jays meeting in the garden,
arranging a promenade over air and to the Spree.
To take the tram nowhere (nowhere to go) and feel
its minute vibrations as it rounds off Frankfurter Allee
and barrels to Scharnweberstrasse, clean echo, tram naught,
stone soft . . . the complicated rumble of its wheels.
I can feel it before I hear it, hear it before I see it.

Though the stop is only another few feet, you will not meet it.
And the walk to the river, to the neighborhood beyond,
will be better for you. Much of your life is accomplished
within a quarter-mile of your bedroom.
Autumn lasts two weeks.

Circumferential train; bisecting train;
city-supported orange daily train; the private train.

It Is Good

Below the moon of paradise
our lord caught Adam maundering
and laid by him another soul
not that she would his soul entice
            but gladness to them bring.

They stood together on the earth
and from its stone their corn they coaxed.
Adam and stream were part and whole
made doubly whole in silent mirth
            and the green became the oaks.

Many are wonders I have seen:
queer the rain and the hollow sky,
black the donkey, brown the coal,
for you and I a tone beteem
            and a tone will flutter by.

Notes

"A Quality of Portugal" and "Diptych" first appeared in *Lana Turner*; "Aeschylus," "For Ben," "46th Street and West Avenue," and "Epigraphs" at *Petri Press*; "Honest James," "Her Poems," "On Finishing *The Narrative of Arthur Gordon Pym*," "The New Tendency," and "The Three Men in the One Garden" in *Company*.

"Pennsylvania" responds to a lyric of Jake Fournier's, beginning: *Horsechestnut trees / with palmate leaves . . . .*

The poems in Section II, and the epigraph to Section I, depart from poems of Goethe's. Some, or parts of some, lie close to the original German text, others quite far away. All, with the exception of "The Four Seasons," were found initially in *Goethe: Selected Verse*, ed. David Luke, New York: Penguin, 1981. "Vier Jahreszeiten" is included in *Goethe: Gedichte*, Frankfurt a.M.: Insel, 1982. The Luke volume contains "plain prose translations," consulted sparingly and departed from liberally.

I thank those who read the manuscript in its stages, or looked at poems as they arose: Sara Deniz Akant, Micah Bateman, Ben Estes, Alan Felsenthal, Jake Fournier, Mark Gaioni, Jessica Laser, Hannah Loeb, Ted Mathys, Kiley McLaughlin, Andrew Nance, Dan Poppick, Adrienne Raphel, Alex Walton, John Ashbery, Cal Bedient, James Galvin, Mark Levine, Dora Malech, Jennifer

Moxley, Cole Swensen, and Susan Wheeler. Many poems were discussed in workshop at the University of Iowa, and I am indebted to my teachers and fellow students for their insights. Special thanks to Mary Austin Speaker, for her marvelous book design, and to everyone at The Song Cave. For Mary Pearsall's encouragement I am forever grateful. To my father, mother, and brother I give my love.

OTHER TITLES FROM THE SONG CAVE:

1. *A Dark Dreambox of Another Kind*, by **Alfred Starr Hamilton**
2. *My Enemies*, by **Jane Gregory**
3. *Rude Woods*, by **Nate Klug**
4. *Georges Braque and Others*, by **Trevor Winkfield**
5. *The Living Method*, by **Sara Nicholson**
6. *Splash State*, by **Todd Colby**
7. *Essay Stanzas*, by **Thomas Meyer**
8. *Illustrated Games of Patience*, by **Ben Estes**
9. *Dark Green*, by **Emily Hunt**